completed the
Winter 2012
Stories in Art Series

National Gallery of Art

Education Division

THE USBORNE

ART
TREASURY

With original artwork by Vincent van Gogh,
Katsushika Hokusai, Hendrick Avercamp,
Pablo Picasso, unknown African artists,
Paul Klee, Henri Rousseau, Alexander Calder,
Henri Matisse, James Whistler, Claude Monet,
Vassily Kandinsky, Shen Quan, Edgar Degas,
Alberto Giacometti, Damien Hirst,
Johnny Bulunbulun, Georgia O'Keeffe,
Jackson Pollock, unknown Iranian artists,
JMW Turner and Richard Long

Project artwork by Abigail Brown,
Nicola Butler, Mary Cartwright, Katie Lovell,
Sam Meredith, and Non and Daisy Taylor
Step artwork by Molly Sage
Cartoons by Georgien Overwater

Edited by Abigail Wheatley and Jane Chisholm
American editor: Carrie Armstrong
Managing designer: Mary Cartwright
Picture research by Ruth King
Digital manipulation by John Russell

THE USBORNE

ART

TREASURY

Rosie Dickins

Designed by Nicola Butler

With thanks to Dr. Erika Langmuir, OBE
for expert information and advice

Contents

Introduction

This book has a fascinating collection of art from around the world. It has masks from Africa, prints from Japan, and paintings and sculptures from Europe. You can read about each work of art and the artist who made it, and then try out a project inspired by it. Some of the projects show you how to use the same method or materials. Other projects are based on what the artwork shows, so you can explore the same themes and ideas.

Water Lilies - Morning

painted by Claude Monet between 1914 and 1918

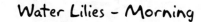

This picture is one of a series, designed to line a room, showing the pond from dawn to dusk.

This calm scene shows the pond in Claude Monet's garden at Giverny in France. Monet designed the pond himself, and painted it again and again over thirty years. He filled huge canvases with rapid dabs of paint, trying to capture the effect of sunlight on water. His loose, sketchy style creates a dreamy atmosphere, full of ripples, reflections and glowing lilies.

About Monet

Claude Monet was born in France in 1840. As a young artist, he spent most of his time painting outdoors - whether it was sunny fields, windy beaches or snowy roads. Whatever the weather, he wanted to be on the spot to study the changing light.

At first, people laughed at Monet's style. They thought his pictures were far too rough and sketchy. But, by the time he died in 1926, he was one of the world's most successful artists, with whole galleries devoted to his work.

Monet would go to great lengths to get the perfect view. He sat on rocking boats, climbed rickety ladders and even dug trenches to stand in.

48

49

Read about a famous water lily picture, built up out of layers of paint - then try making your own lilies using layers of colored tissue paper.

What you will need

Most artists work in studios, where they have space to make and store things. But a table or floor covered in newspaper, and a box for your art materials, will do just as well. It's a good idea to read through each activity before you start, to make sure you have everything you will need. Here is a list of the materials used in the projects in this book:

* Colored paper, plain paper and tissue paper
* Giftwrap and newspaper
* Cardboard, felt and scraps of fabric
* Pencils, felt-tip pens and ink
* Chalks or chalk pastels
* Wax crayons and oil pastels
* Watercolor paint
* Acrylic paint and poster paint
* Paint brushes in different sizes
* Craft glue, clear tape and a glue stick
* Silver foil, glitter and string or raffia
* A plastic fork and a drinking straw
* A paper plate, a cardboard box and a pin
* Cotton balls, pipe cleaners and poster putty
* A sponge, a toothpick and some salt
* Polystyrene from packaging

The Starry Night

painted by Vincent van Gogh in 1889

Van Gogh once said, "looking at the stars always makes me dream."

This picture shows a dramatic night sky with twinkling stars and twisting trees. The scene has been built up out of layers of paint so thick, you can see the brush marks in it. The artist, Vincent van Gogh, liked to use strongly colored paint, often straight from the tube. His intense colors and swirling brush strokes make his pictures vivid and full of movement.

About van Gogh

Vincent van Gogh was born in Holland in 1853. By the age of 27, he had tried teaching, shop work and preaching, all without success. Then, he decided to devote himself to art. But he struggled to make a living and managed to sell only one painting during his life. Today his pictures are worth millions.

Sadly, van Gogh suffered from mental illness. In one famous incident, he cut off part of his left ear after arguing with a friend. By 1889, he was in a mental hospital. He continued to paint furiously, but became more and more depressed. A year later, he shot himself.

Swirly landscape

Vincent van Gogh created his landscape with dramatic swirls and curls built up of thick layers of paint. You can try this swirly technique for yourself using thick acrylic paints.

The glue makes the paint thicker.

1. On thick paper, sketch a landscape with rolling hills, leafy trees and a swirling, cloudy sky.

2. Squeeze out some acrylic paints onto a plate. Mix a few drops of craft glue into each blob.

3. Paint blue and white swirls for a cloudy sky. Don't worry if you go over the lines of your sketch.

You could scrape some short lines to look like grass.

4. Scrape a plastic fork around the curves of the clouds and sky, to make swirly marks in the paint.

5. Paint hills and trees in browns, greens and yellows. Wipe the fork, then scrape wavy lines along the hills.

6. Finally, use the tip of a paintbrush handle to scrape round curls into the tree tops.

The Great Wave
off Kanagawa

created by Katsushika Hokusai between 1823 and 1829

This print was made by carving a picture onto wooden blocks – one block for each color. The blocks were then coated with ink and pressed onto paper.

This Japanese print is full of drama, with tiny boats being tossed on stormy seas. A huge wave is about to crash over the boats, claws of foam reaching for the sailors. The wave is so big, it seems to dwarf the distant peak of Mount Fuji.

Floating World

In Japan, scenes like this are known as ukiyo-e, or "pictures of the floating world." They are meant to celebrate the fragile beauty of ordinary life. Often, they show popular actors, fashionable women or landscapes with people going about their daily lives, such as these sailors.

About Hokusai

Katsushika Hokusai was born in Tokyo in 1760. He was apprenticed to a printmaker, but experimented so much he was thrown out. Stubbornly, he kept on experimenting and became very successful. In fact, his most popular prints sold so many copies that the blocks used to make them wore out.

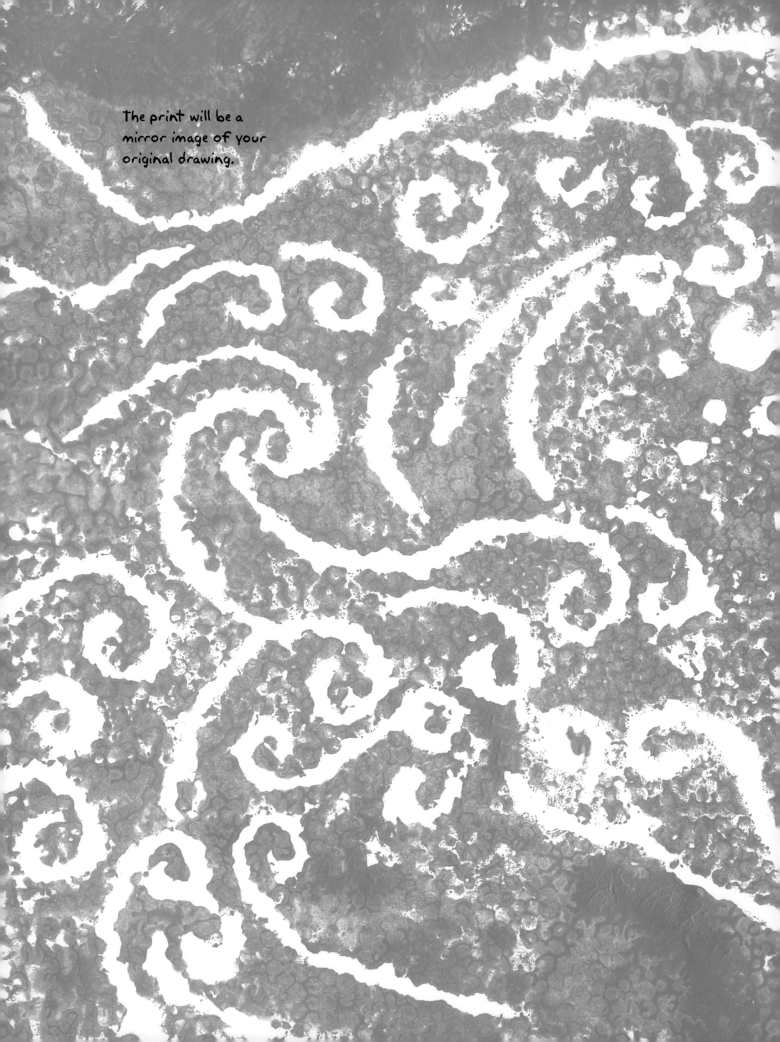

The print will be a mirror image of your original drawing.

Sea print

Hokusai printed his towering wave using sea-blue inks on white paper. These steps show you how you can create your own stormy sea print in blue and white.

Draw big, curly waves.

1. Draw a sea scene on a flat piece of polystyrene from a take-out box or some protective packaging.

2. 'Carve' the scene by pushing a sharp pencil into the sheet. Do this many times along each line.

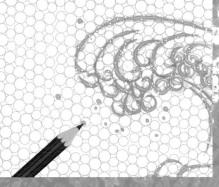

3. Dot some holes around the edges of the waves. Brush off any loose pieces of polystyrene.

4. Mix some blue poster paint and sponge it over the polystyrene. Lay a piece of paper on top.

5. Rub all over the paper with your hand, keeping your fingers flat. Then, lift off the paper.

A Winter Scene with Skaters near a Castle

painted by Hendrick Avercamp in about 1608-09

This 400-year-old Dutch painting shows a busy winter landscape. All kinds of people are out walking in the snow or skating across the ice – or falling over. There is even a snowball fight going on.

Imaginary castles

At the time of this picture, there was a craze for landscape paintings. The artist, Hendrick Avercamp, specialized in winter scenes. He lived in Holland and based his pictures on the countryside and people around him. The result looks incredibly lifelike, but it isn't all real. The castle with the pink tower existed only in Avercamp's imagination.

These close-ups show some of the skaters in more detail. Notice their bulky winter clothes.

About Avercamp

Hendrick Avercamp was born in the Netherlands in 1585 and spent most of his life in the sleepy little Dutch town of Kampen. He was known as the 'mute of Kampen' because he was deaf and never learned to speak. But his disability didn't stop him from studying art in Amsterdam and selling his pictures across Europe.

Winter trees

Bare trees tower over Avercamp's picture, making it feel cold and wintry. This project shows you how to create your own winter trees using runny paint and a drinking straw.

1. Mix some runny blue watercolor paint and brush it onto a piece of white paper, for a sky.

2. Before the paint dries, dip a brush in water and let it drip over the sky, to spread the paint.

3. Mix some runny brown watercolor paint. Paint the ground, leaving white patches showing.

Blow small blobs
of paint to make
clumps of grass.

4. When the paint is dry,
mix some runny dark
brown watercolor paint.
Dab a blob on the ground.

5. Blow on the blob
through a drinking
straw, so the paint flows
up and makes a trunk.

6. Use the end of the
straw to pull lines of
paint out of the trunk.
Blow them into branches.

19

Punchinello with a Guitar

painted by Pablo Picasso in 1920

This colorful painting shows a clown in a baggy white suit and conical hat, stepping onto a stage with a guitar. He hasn't been drawn in a lifelike way, but is made up of geometric shapes. The title tells you his name – Punchinello – a traditional Italian character, better known as Mr. Punch from "Punch and Judy" puppet shows.

Clowning around

The artist, Pablo Picasso, loved clowns and circuses. According to friends, he went to the circus every week and knew many of the performers well. There are circus characters, especially clowns and acrobats, in many of his pictures.

About Picasso

Pablo Picasso was born in Spain in 1881. He began drawing even before he could talk, and his father, who was an art teacher, encouraged his natural talent. During his life Picasso created over 20,000 works of art and became one of the world's most famous artists. There are several museums dedicated to his work.

Picasso helping his son to draw

21

Clown collage

Picasso made dozens of clown pictures and invented the technique of collage (gluing things onto his pictures). This project shows you how to make your own blocky clown collage, using different papers and fabrics.

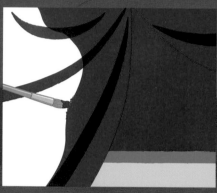

1. On a piece of thick paper, paint a stage and a curtain. Leave it to dry.

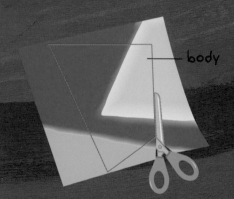

2. From paper or fabric, cut a half-circle head, and a blocky body like this.

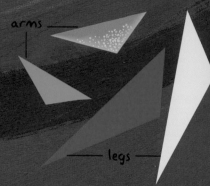

3. Cut out two triangles for arms, two for legs and four tiny ones for hands and feet.

4. Cut out a curvy ruff, like this, and a half-circle and a triangle for a hat.

5. Arrange the pieces on top of the painted stage and glue them down.

6. Stick on more cut-out shapes for decoration. Add details with a felt-tip pen.

Mix materials - such as painted
newspaper, giftwrap or felt -
for different patterns and textures.

23

African masks

made by unknown artists
in Africa in the 19th century

Elaborately carved and
decorated masks have been
made in Africa for thousands of
years. We don't know the names
of the artists, but creating masks was
a highly respected skill. The artists
had to know all about working
with wood and about many
different masks.

The masks show the faces of
spirits – usually a god, an
ancestor or an animal. Artists
had to carve and paint each
mask in a particular way, so people
knew which spirit it was meant to
be. They believed that if you put
on a mask, the spirit it showed
would enter your body.

This wooden spirit mask was created
by the Songye people. The large round
crest was meant to hold magic powers.

24

Making masks

Traditionally, masks were worn during important ceremonies, such as harvest festivals and funerals. Many young people wore masks to go through secret rites marking the end of their childhood. The mask ceremonies were full of drama and music. The mask wearers would perform ritual dances, stamping and clapping, and sometimes speaking for the spirits of the masks.

Often, dancers wore elaborate costumes with their masks.

This wood and straw mask was made by the Kuba people to represent one of their ancestors.

Cardboard mask

African masks are carved in wood and carefully decorated. This project shows you how to make your own mask by cutting and decorating thick, corrugated cardboard from a box.

You can buy raffia from arts and craft stores, florists or garden centers.

Cut out shapes like these to decorate your mask.

You could draw around a big plate, then trim the sides.

1. Draw a simple face shape on some corrugated cardboard and cut it out. Bend it into a curve.

2. Draw two dots about halfway down. Carefully push a sharp pencil through the card to make eyeholes.

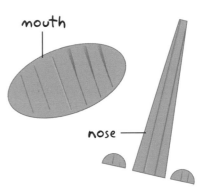

mouth

nose

3. From more cardboard, cut a long triangle and two half-circles for a nose, and an oval for a mouth.

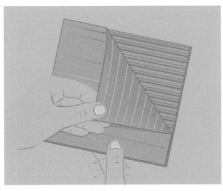

4. Peel the top layer off some more cardboard. Cut out two half-ovals for eyes, from the bumpy part.

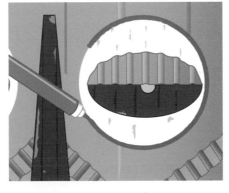

5. Cut out more shapes. Glue all the shapes onto the mask and decorate it with paint or felt-tip pens.

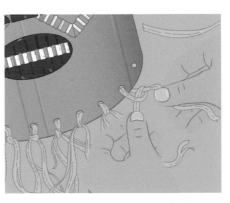

6. Make holes around the chin. Poke short pieces of raffia or string through the holes and knot them on.

The Golden Fish

painted by Paul Klee in 1925

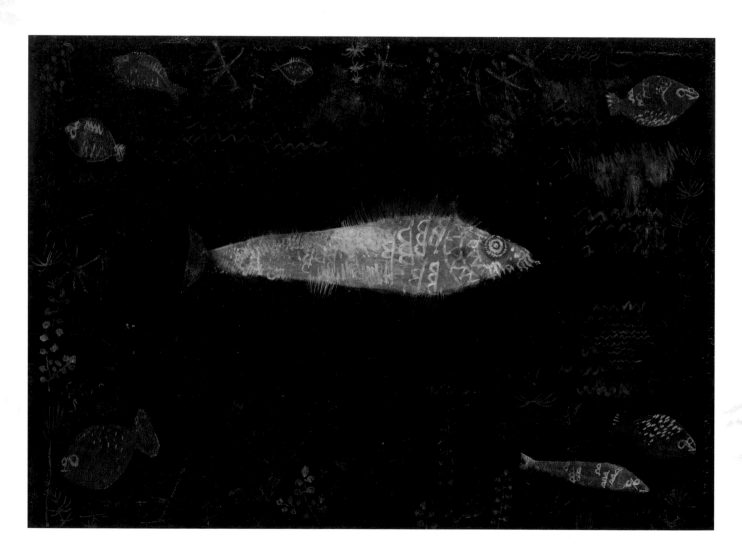

This picture was painted using two kinds of paints: watercolors and oil paints.
Watercolors are thinner and good for see-through effects.
Oil paints are thicker and good for vivid colors.

This fishy painting is filled with imaginary sea life, but all the focus is on the big golden fish in the middle. The small fish and plants cluster around the edges, like a decorative border.

Mysterious meanings

The golden fish is no ordinary sea creature. It glows strangely in the dark, making it look magical and mysterious. And the lines and squiggles around it look like some kind of secret, ancient writing.

The artist, Paul Klee, wasn't interested in painting the things around him, because he thought art should be about ideas, beliefs and feelings. So he filled his pictures with strange symbols and fragments of writing designed to suggest another, more magical world.

These symbols were used in ancient Egyptian writing.

About Klee

Paul Klee was born in Switzerland in 1879. He was a gifted violinist and almost became a musician, but he chose to study art instead. He lived and worked in Germany until the 1930s, when the Nazis came to power. The Nazis hated a lot of modern art, including Klee's. They claimed it was "degenerate" or corrupt, and banned it. Klee was forced to return to Switzerland. Soon after, he fell seriously ill with a rare disease, and died in 1940.

Magical creatures

Paul Klee created magical fish pictures using watercolor and oil paints. You can create a similar effect with watercolor paints and oil pastels or wax crayons.

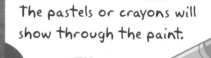

The pastels or crayons will show through the paint.

1. Lightly sketch some sea creatures on thick white paper. Add some plants and squiggles around them.

2. Fill in the creatures with bright oil pastels or wax crayons. Draw over the plants and squiggles, too.

3. Mix some watercolor paint in shades of dark blue and paint it over the entire scene, using a big brush.

Monkeys in an Orange Grove

painted by Henri Rousseau in 1910

Rousseau created his jungles out of the things around him. Some of his tropical plants were based on houseplants.

This glowing jungle scene was painted by French artist Henri Rousseau. He loved creating tropical pictures, but he had never actually seen a jungle. Instead, he painted from sketches he made in local parks and zoos. The results were beautifully decorative, if not very lifelike. Here, the plants grow in orderly rows, not tangled together like real jungle – but they still look lush and inviting.

About Rousseau

Henri Rousseau was born in France in 1844 and never went to art school. He worked as a customs officer in Paris, and painted in his spare time. At first, art critics laughed at his simple, self-taught style. But many artists admired it. They felt that Rousseau's pictures had a strange, dreamlike quality that more sophisticated artists couldn't imitate.

Rousseau in his Paris studio

You could add a jungle animal based on a sketch of your pet.

Jungle scene

R ousseau used glowing colors and strong shadows to bring his jungle painting to life. Now you can create your own jungle, with dramatic shading and brightly colored fruit.

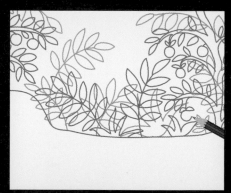

1. On a piece of thick pale blue paper, draw a jungle scene with overlapping branches, leaves and fruit.

2. Mix some watercolor paint in dark green and fill in some of the branches and leaves.

3. Let the paint dry. Then, fill in the rest of the leaves and branches, and the ground, with black ink.

Fill in the top half of the leaf.

4. When the ink is dry, mix some orange watercolor paint and fill in the fruit. Wait until that dries, too.

5. Draw a line along the middle of every black leaf, using a dark green pencil. Shade in half of each leaf.

6. Shade half of each green leaf with a light green pencil. Outline the oranges in red pencil and add dots.

Eleven Polychrome

This artwork gets its name from the eleven multi-colored or "polychrome" shapes.

created by Alexander Calder
in 1956

Nowadays, mobiles are mass-produced and sold in stores around the world. But, in the 1930s, they were a brand new idea. The inspiration came from an artist named Alexander Calder. He wanted to create sculptures that moved – but without machinery. The result was the first mobile.

Catching the breeze

This mobile is designed to hang in mid-air and catch the breeze. It is made of moving branches tipped with metal shapes. The branches are heavy, but their weight is balanced so it takes only the slightest breath of wind to make them drift and turn.

Calder once said, "To most people who look at a mobile, it's no more than a series of flat objects that move. To a few, though, it may be poetry."

About Calder

Alexander Calder was born in America in 1898. He came from a family of artists and he set up his own workshop at the age of eight, making tiny moving animals out of metal. Although he studied to be an engineer, he soon returned to art. He is best known for his mobiles, but he also made fixed sculptures, which he called "stabiles."

One of Calder's first grown-up works of art was a toy circus with moving performers.

Hanging mobile

Alexander Calder created huge mobiles out of painted steel and wire. This project shows you how to make a miniature version using cardboard and pipe cleaners.

Use the shorter pipe cleaners lower down.

1. Take six different-sized pipe cleaners and bend the ends down to make curved "arms" like this.

2. Take one arm and bend one end around to make a loop. Thread a second arm through the loop, like this.

3. Add five of the arms in the same way. When you thread on the bottom arm, don't loop its ends.

Make seven matching pairs of shapes like this.

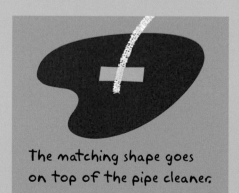

The matching shape goes on top of the pipe cleaner.

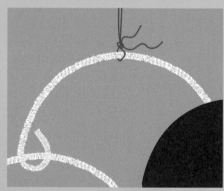

4. Fold some thick paper in half. Draw a curvy shape, then cut around it, through both layers of paper.

5. Tape one shape under the free end of an arm. Glue the matching shape on top. Do this six more times.

6. Loop string around the top arm and hang up the mobile. Bend the arms around until they balance.

Hang your mobile
somewhere it can
move in the breeze.

39

the Sorrows of the King

created by Henri Matisse in 1952

This cut-paper collage shows a king sitting on a raised platform, playing a guitar. Another musician crouches at his feet and a woman dances before them. The colorful patterns create a cheerful effect – like the music and dancing, which are meant to distract the king from his sorrows.

Drawing with scissors

Henri Matisse became famous for his paintings. But when he made this picture, he was too ill to stand up at an easel and paint. Instead, he began to create scenes with shapes cut out of paper. He called this "drawing with scissors," but it is usually known as collage.

This photograph shows Matisse in bed, cutting out shapes for a picture.

About Matisse

Henri Matisse was born in 1869 in France. He was going to be a lawyer, but then became ill. While he was recovering, his mother bought him a box of paints to keep him entertained – and he was hooked. As soon as he was well again, he gave up law and trained to become an artist.

Colorful collage

Henri Matisse loved making colorful pictures about music and movement. You can create your own version with this cheerful collage.

1. Cut out some large rectangles from colorful paper, such as old magazines or giftwrap.

2. Glue the rectangles onto a sheet of paper, so they overlap and cover it completely.

saxophone

end piece

3. Draw a wavy saxophone shape and an oval end piece, like this. Carefully cut around the shapes.

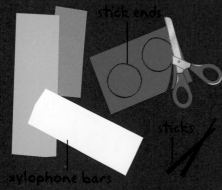

stick ends

xylophone bars

sticks

4. Cut out small rectangles to make a xylophone. For xylophone sticks, cut two thin strips and two circles.

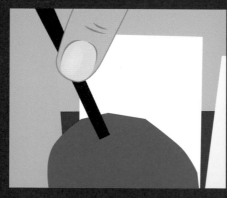

5. Arrange the instruments on top of your picture and glue them down. Glue the xylophone sticks on last.

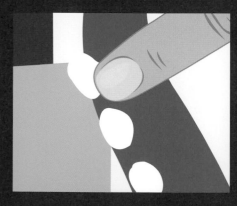

6. Draw some tiny oval shapes. Cut them out and glue them onto the saxophone to make its keys.

Try adding stars and
wavy strips around
the instruments,
to suggest sounds.

Nocturne in Black and Gold (the Falling Rocket)

painted by James Abbott McNeill Whistler in 1875

This dark, moody painting conjures up the thrill and excitement of a firework display. Puffs of smoke and trails of glowing, golden sparks fill the night sky. A cluster of dark shapes on the left might be a watching crowd, but it's too blurry to make out much else.

Flinging paint

This picture led to a bitter fight between the artist, James Whistler, and an art critic named John Ruskin. Ruskin hated the picture. He thought it was far too messy and sloppily painted, and accused Whistler of "flinging a pot of paint in the public's face."

In reply, Whistler snapped that a picture's value didn't depend on how long he had spent painting it, but on his skill with a brush. He was so angry he took Ruskin to court, to try to make him pay for the insult. He won, but got only a quarter of a penny. After paying his lawyers, Whistler was left with almost no money. But he wore the quarter penny on his watch chain for the rest of his life.

About Whistler

James Whistler was born in America in 1834. At first he planned to be an army officer, but he failed the exams, so he moved to France and took up art. Later, he spent many years working in London. He had huge success with his peaceful, atmospheric style of painting – though he was known for his hot temper and fell out with some of his best clients.

Spattery fireworks

Whistler conjured up the feel of a firework display out of a smudge of smoke and a scatter of bright sparks. You can recreate this effect using sponged and spattered paint.

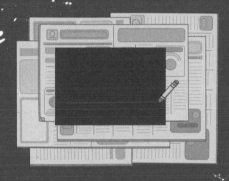

1. Draw a low horizon line on a piece of purple paper. Lay your paper on plenty of newspaper.

2. Use a sponge to dab some pink and orange poster paint in patches above and below the line.

3. Rinse the sponge. Press its flat side into dark purple paint, then print a blocky shape above the line.

4. Print more blocky shapes above and below the horizon line, for buildings and their reflections.

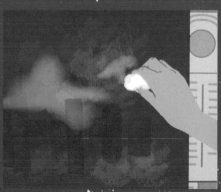

5. When the paint is dry, use a cotton ball to smudge on purple and yellow chalk pastel or chalk, for smoke.

6. Mix some runny paint in yellows and reds. Dip in a brush, hold it over the paper and flick the bristles.

Water Lilies – Morning

painted by Claude Monet between 1914 and 1918

This calm scene shows the pond in Claude Monet's garden at Giverny in France. Monet designed the pond himself, and painted it again and again over thirty years. He filled huge canvases with rapid dabs of paint, trying to capture the effect of sunlight on water. His loose, sketchy style creates a dreamy atmosphere, full of ripples, reflections and glowing lilies.

This picture is one of a series, designed to line a room, showing the pond from dawn to dusk.

About Monet

Claude Monet was born in France in 1840. As a young artist, he spent most of his time painting outdoors – whether it was sunny fields, windy beaches or snowy roads. Whatever the weather, he wanted to be on the spot to study the changing light.

At first, people laughed at Monet's style. They thought his pictures were far too rough and sketchy. But, by the time he died in 1926, he was one of the world's most successful artists, with whole galleries devoted to his work.

Monet would go to great lengths to get the perfect view. He sat on rocking boats, climbed rickety ladders and even dug trenches to stand in.

49

Layered lilies

Monet created his lily pictures using layers of white and colored paint. You can get a similar effect using layers of colored tissue paper on white paper.

1. Tear some big strips of blue tissue paper, and some smaller strips of green and lilac.

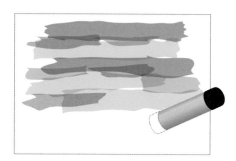

2. Overlap and glue the strips across a piece of thick white paper, to make a pond.

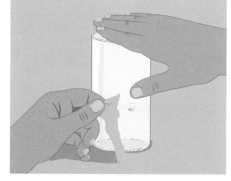

3. Place a glass over some green tissue paper and tear around it to make a circle. Make several.

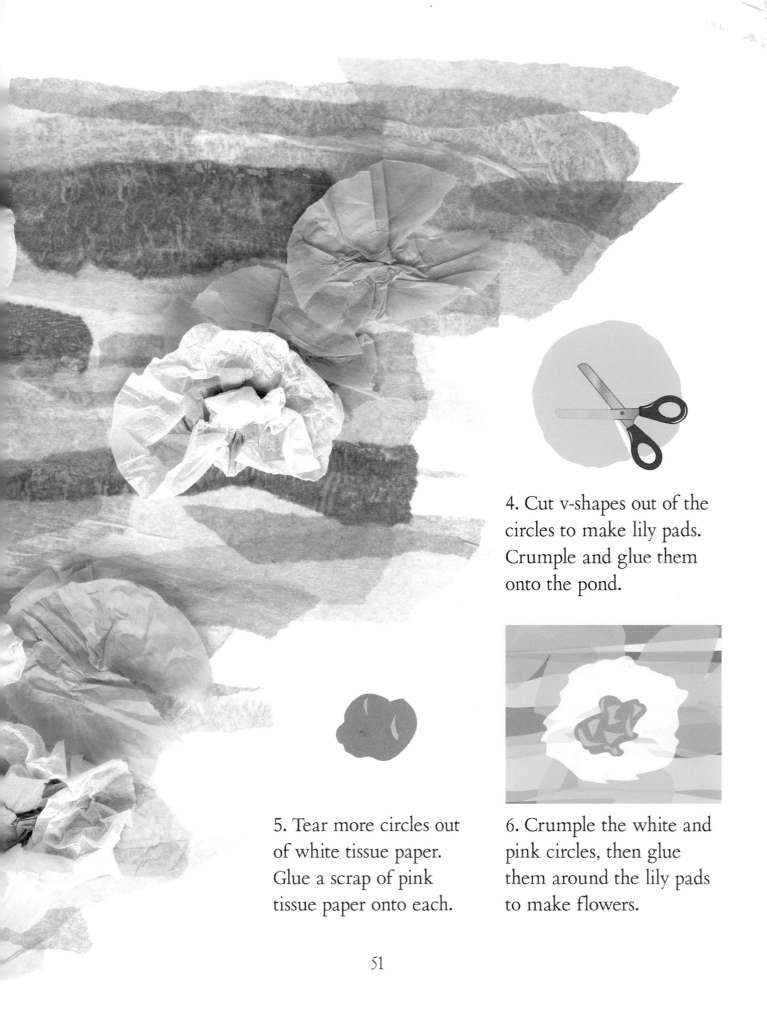

4. Cut v-shapes out of the circles to make lily pads. Crumple and glue them onto the pond.

5. Tear more circles out of white tissue paper. Glue a scrap of pink tissue paper onto each.

6. Crumple the white and pink circles, then glue them around the lily pads to make flowers.

51

Squares with Concentric Circles

painted by Vassily Kandinsky in 1913

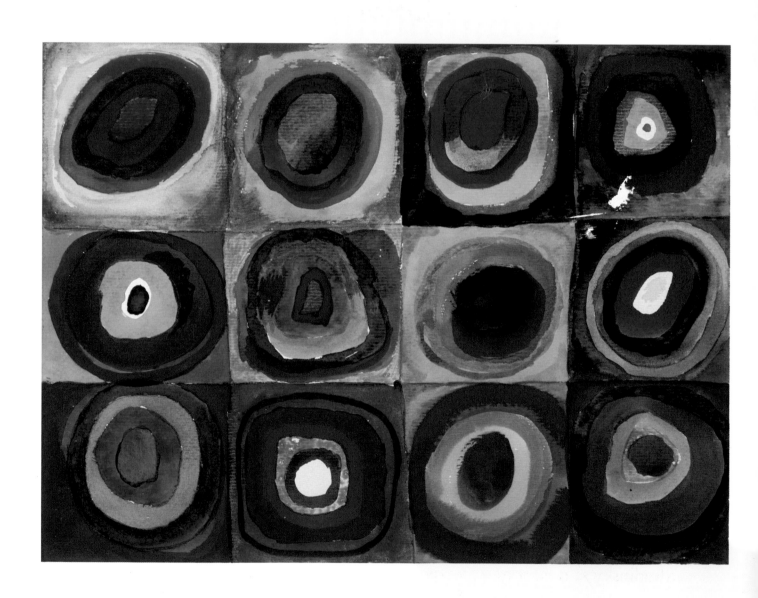

This bold, colorful picture was painted by Russian artist Vassily Kandinsky, to explore the effect of placing different colors side by side. He wanted to find out which colors stand out and which ones blend together, and how to balance different colors to create a bright, attractive pattern.

Color and feeling

Color was incredibly important to Kandinsky. He believed colors could express feelings in the same way as music. According to him, "Color is a power that directly influences the soul... Color is the keyboard... the artist is the hand that plays." He felt the effect of colors so strongly, he even claimed that looking at colors made him hear musical sounds.

About Kandinsky

Kandinsky was born in Russia in 1866, into a musical family. He started off as a lawyer – it wasn't until he was in his thirties that he took up painting. He was one of the first artists to develop "abstract" art – art that doesn't try to show actual objects, people or scenes.

Kandinsky said he began to experiment after seeing a picture that had fallen on its side. Seen sideways, he didn't recognize it. Instead, he saw an abstract arrangement of shapes and colors, and found that much more interesting.

Color contrasts

Kandinsky created a striking picture using circles in contrasting colors. Try it for yourself using watercolor paints and oil pastels or wax crayons.

Fold

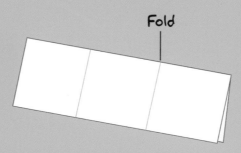

1. Fold a piece of paper into three equal sections, like this. Pinch the creases, then unfold the paper.

2. Then, fold the paper in half lengthways. Pinch the crease and unfold it. The creases make six squares.

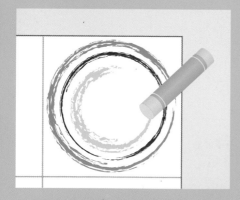

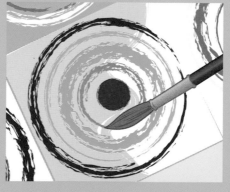

3. Using oil pastels or wax crayons, draw some rings inside each square. Leave gaps between the rings.

4. Paint over the squares with watercolor paint, using a different color for each square.

The oil pastels or wax crayons show through the paint and create colorful contrasts.

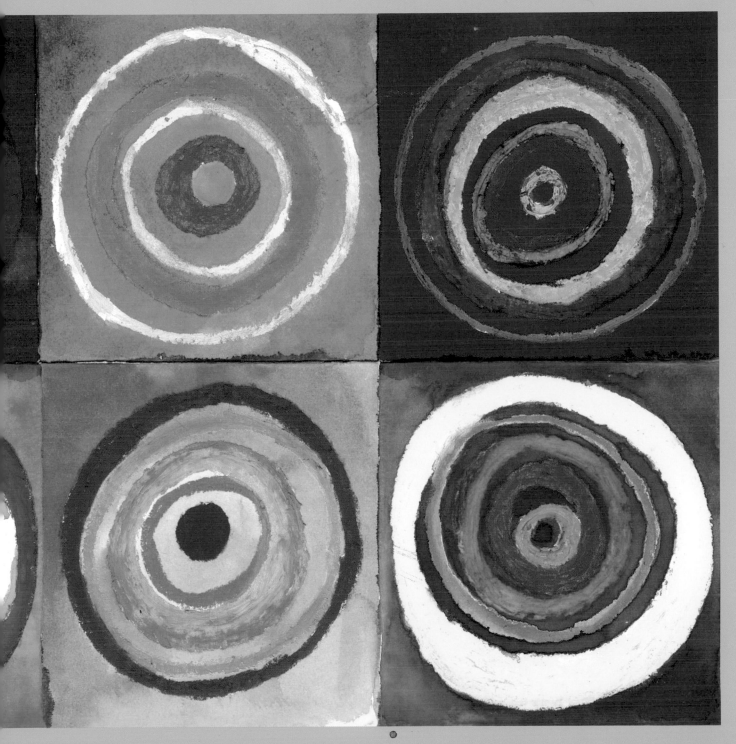

Cat

painted by Shen Quan in 1747

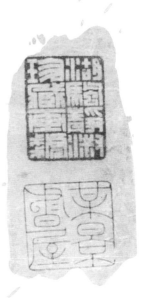

This picture from China shows a cat staring intently at two bees. Down the side, there is a line of flowing Chinese writing which says: "Painted one autumn, in the reign of Emperor Qianlong, by Shen Quan." The red stamps beside and below the writing are the official marks or "seals" of the artist Shen Quan and the owner of the picture.

Sweeps and strokes

Like most Chinese paintings, this scene was created using a soft, animal-hair brush and watery ink, and it was painted fast, with rapid sweeps and strokes. Chinese artists spend years practicing the precise movements used to create particular shapes and effects.

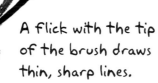

A flick with the tip of the brush draws thin, sharp lines.

A firm, smooth brush stroke gives thick, dark lines.

A sideways dab of the brush makes a neat leaf or petal shape.

About Shen Quan

Shen Quan was born in China in 1682. He was a famous scholar, admired for his music and poetry as well as his pictures. He specialized in scenes of animals and flowers, painted in a very detailed, lifelike way. By comparison, this cat is fairly roughly sketched and was probably painted just for fun.

Cat painting

This project shows you how to paint your own Chinese-style cat, using a soft, round brush and ink like Shen Quan. Bottled ink works well, or you can snip the end off an ink cartridge.

1. Mix some watery ink. Paint a small oval cat's head, a large oval body and a curved tail.

2. Paint two straight lines for the front leg and a curved line for the back leg. Add round paws.

3. Give the cat pointed ears. Paint a tree trunk with branches forking off it. Let the ink dry.

4. Dip the very tip of your brush in undiluted ink, then paint the cat's eyes, nose and whiskers.

5. Pressing lightly with the tip of your brush, add some thin twigs and plant stems.

6. For leaves and flowers, roll your brush in ink, then press it sideways onto the paper.

Add some curved markings on the cat's fur to make it look fluffy.

Dancers in Blue

drawn by Edgar Degas in 1897

This delicate pastel picture of four ballet dancers getting ready for a show was drawn by French artist Edgar Degas. He was fascinated by dancers and created over 1,500 pictures and sculptures of them.

Through the keyhole

This picture is like a glimpse backstage, where dancers are checking their costumes and warming up. One dancer holds onto a piece of scenery to steady herself. Another stoops to adjust her shoe and disappears off the bottom of the paper.

Degas once said he wanted to "paint life through a keyhole" – meaning he wanted to capture people as they really looked, rather than in formal poses. And this picture does seem like a quick, on-the-spot sketch. He drew it with swift lines and dabs of color, using light, feathery strokes on the dancers' tutus and more solid shading on their bodies.

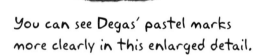

You can see Degas' pastel marks more clearly in this enlarged detail.

About Degas

Edgar Degas was born in France in 1834. He was fascinated by movement and is famous for his pictures of dancers and racehorses. By the time he made this drawing, he was getting old and suffering from eye problems, and rarely left his studio. But he still worked furiously on drawings and sculptures of dancers, based on memory, imagination and earlier sketches.

Pastel dancers

Degas used soft pastels to capture the delicate fabric of his dancers' costumes. You can use chalk pastels or chalks to create a similar effect.

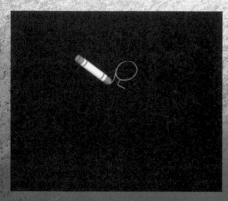

1. On rough brown or black paper, sketch an oval head and a curved neck in chalk pastel or chalk.

2. Draw on a triangular body and a wide, round ballet dancer's skirt. Add some gently curving arms.

3. Color in the skin and add pink cheeks. Smooth over the skin tones with your finger.

Color the background too.

4. Fill in the dress with shades of blue, green and lilac. Work out from the waist, using short strokes.

5. Finally, add some sleeves, hair, eyes and lips, and any small details like roses and flowing ribbons.

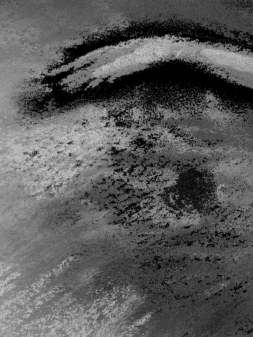

You could add legs with
pointed ballet shoes,
if you have space.

The Square

created by Alberto Giacometti in 1949

✝his sculpture shows five people walking across a city square. They don't seem to be talking to each other, just passing through. And there isn't much to tell them apart. They all have scrawny, stick-like bodies and huge, heavy feet. It is as if the artist was trying to suggest how lonely and anonymous life can be in cities.

Different views

The artist, Alberto Giacometti, made several versions of this sculpture, placing the people in different positions each time. He said he loved to watch people walking in the street, and how "they unceasingly form and reform living compositions..."

About Giacometti

Alberto Giacometti was born in Switzerland in 1901. He wasn't the only artist in his family – his father painted and his brother sculpted. For a while, Giacometti made very, very tiny sculptures. Even after four years, all his work fit into six matchboxes. Then he tried making things bigger, producing stick figures like these, for which he became famous. People admired the way they seemed to capture the pain and uncertainty of modern life.

The sculpture was made of bronze and polished to give it a dark, shiny finish. Each figure is only about 8in high.

Foil Figures

Alberto Giacometti sculpted hundreds of stick people in different poses. You can sculpt your own stick people using pipe cleaners and foil.

twist here

twist here

1. Twist the ends of two pipe cleaners together to make a pair of legs. Keep twisting to form a body.

2. Crumple up a small ball of paper. Loop the middle of another pipe cleaner over the ball and twist it tight.

3. Place this piece at the top of the body for a head and arms. Wind each arm twice around the body.

4. Roll two balls of poster putty and push the legs into them. Squash them so the figure stands up.

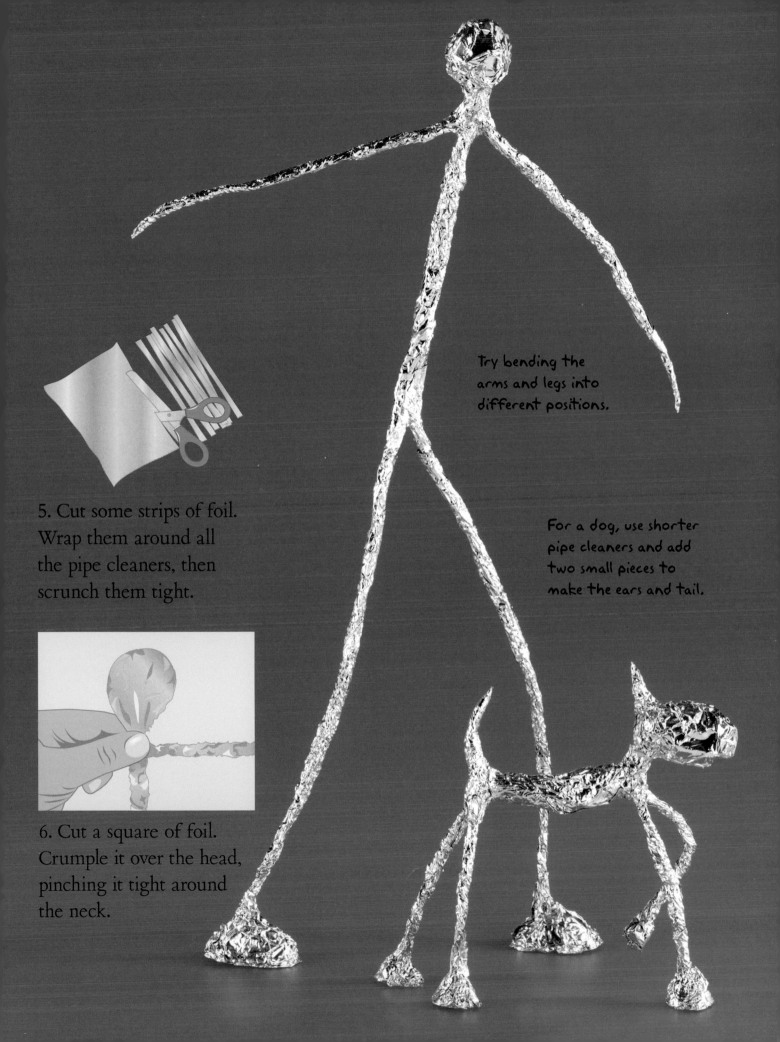

5. Cut some strips of foil. Wrap them around all the pipe cleaners, then scrunch them tight.

6. Cut a square of foil. Crumple it over the head, pinching it tight around the neck.

Try bending the arms and legs into different positions.

For a dog, use shorter pipe cleaners and add two small pieces to make the ears and tail.

Spin painting

created by Damien Hirst in 1995

Hirst named this picture: "beautiful, sharp, screaming, subtle, ice-cream-ish, yikes, gosh with pinks painting (with rosy orange center)".

This picture was made by pouring runny paint onto a big spinning canvas. As the paint splashed down, the spinning motion made the drips flow outwards and create a streaky pattern. The artist, Damien Hirst, said he was inspired to try this technique by a children's television program he had seen years before.

Spin doctors

Some art critics have complained that spin pictures aren't real art. And it's true that splashing and spinning might seem like a rather haphazard way of painting. But the results aren't all down to chance. The artist still has to choose which colors to use, how to pour them and when to stop. He also has to choose how to display the finished picture. Hirst likes to show his spin pictures turning, so they can be seen every way up.

About Hirst

Damien Hirst was born in England in 1965. At school, his art grades were bad, but he managed to secure a place at art college after two attempts. While there, he organized some hugely successful exhibitions. He was offered a job running an art gallery, but he turned it down to concentrate on making his own art. One of his best-known works is a dead shark floating in a tank of preservative. But his paintings are probably more popular – regular grids of colored dots and colorful spin pictures.

Spin-painted plate

Damien Hirst creates his spin pictures on a huge wheel. You can try a similar technique by spinning a paper plate. It's very messy – so watch out for flying paint.

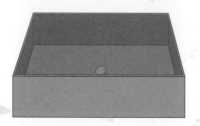
The box will help to catch any flying drips of paint.

Push the pin in from the front of the plate.

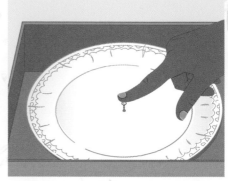

1. Find a shallow cardboard box, bigger than a paper plate. Stick a ball of poster putty in the middle of it.

2. Stick a square of clear tape to the middle of the back of a paper plate. Push a pin through both layers.

3. Put the plate in the box and push the pin into the putty. Try spinning the plate – it may stick at first.

For smaller patches of color flick paint from a brush.

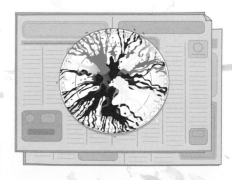

4. Dilute some different colors of poster paint, to make them runny. Dribble some paint over the plate.

5. As the paint falls, spin the plate. Keep dribbling and spinning, using different colors of paint.

6. Lift the plate out of the box and leave it flat on some old newspaper until it is completely dry.

For the finishing touch,
think of a title for your painting.
Does it remind you of anything?

Bark painting

created by Johnny Bulunbulun between 1960 and 1995

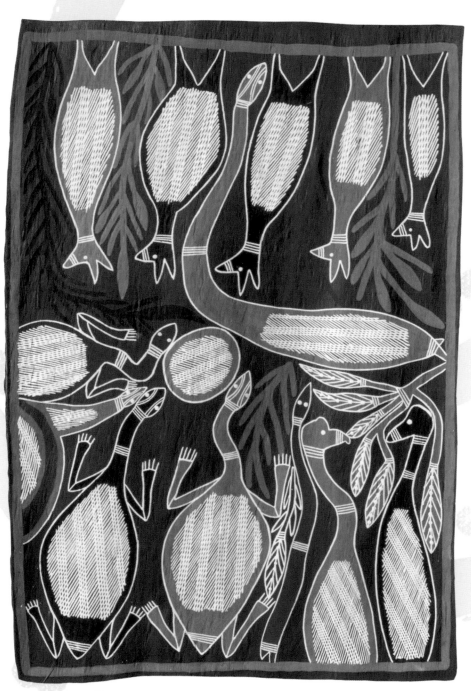

This painting was created on dried tree bark by Aboriginal artist Johnny Bulunbulun. Aboriginal peoples were the first to live in Australia, with a history going back thousands of years. Bulunbulun painted the picture in the traditional Aboriginal way, using natural earth colors and brushes made from twigs or grass.

Sacred art

Bulunbulun's painting reflects Aboriginal beliefs. It shows Australian animals gathering to drink from a waterhole. To Aboriginal peoples, the waterhole is sacred because it represents the source of life. A row of bats hangs from the top of the picture, long-necked turtles and geese gather below, and snakes twist between them. These animals all feature in Aboriginal myths and ceremonies.

About Bulunbulun

Johnny Bulunbulun was born in the 1940s, in a remote part of northern Australia known as Arnhem Land. The land and animals from where he grew up are very important in his work. As well as painting, he is famous for his singing and takes part in traditional Aboriginal ceremonies.

Leave a brown strip showing around the edge.

Scratched animals

Johnny Bulunbulun painted his animals on textured bark. You can get a similar effect by painting onto a torn piece of rough brown paper or cardboard.

Light colors work best.

1. Tear out a rectangular piece of cardboard or paper. Cover it with stripes of color, using oil pastels.

2. Mix some dark acrylic paint with a little water. Then, paint over the pastel so it is completely covered.

Alternatively, you could draw an animal shape first, and just fill that in with pastels and paint.

The oil pastel shows through the scratches.

3. When the paint is almost dry, use a toothpick to scratch different animal shapes and patterns into it.

Jimson Weed

painted by Georgia O'Keeffe in 1932

This painting shows a wild flower known as Jimson weed. In real life, it is a small, bad-smelling flower – another name for it is Stinkwort. Here, though, it seems big and beautiful. In fact, the flower has been enlarged to about fifteen times its real size, creating a picture that measures a huge 48 x 40in.

Small is beautiful

Artist Georgia O'Keeffe painted all kinds of flowers, from ordinary weeds to poppies, lilies, orchids and roses. And she always made them startlingly large, capturing their delicate shapes and colors with smooth, precise brush strokes.

Talking about her flower paintings, O'Keeffe said, "Nobody sees a flower, really, it is so small. We haven't time – and to see takes time... So I said to myself: I'll paint what I see – what the flower is to me – but I'll paint it big... I'll make even busy New Yorkers take time to see what I see of flowers."

About O'Keeffe

Georgia O'Keeffe was born in America in 1887 and grew up on a farm. She always dreamed of being an artist. In 1916, a friend showed some of her drawings to gallery owner Alfred Stieglitz, and he began to display her work. Soon, her paintings were selling for thousands of dollars. O'Keeffe began painting flowers while living in New York City. Later, she moved to New Mexico, where she created stark, beautiful desert scenes. She died in 1986.

Petal collage

Georgia O'Keeffe specialized in smooth, delicate flower pictures. This project shows you how to make a poppy picture using different colors of smooth paper.

1. Fold some red paper in half, and in half again. On the top layer of paper, draw a wide petal shape.

2. Cut around it, through all the layers of paper. Use darker paper to make small petals in the same way.

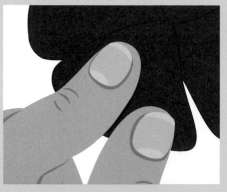

3. Fold some green paper in half. Draw a leaf, like this. Cut around it, through both layers of paper.

4. Arrange the petals and leaves on a large sheet of colored paper. Then, glue them in place.

5. Cut out a small oval and an 'X' in contrasting colors, and glue them in the middle of your flower.

You could add a ring of tiny
drop shapes around the middle
in paper or felt-tip pen.

Lavender Mist

painted by Jackson Pollock in 1950

Pollock originally called this picture "Number 1, 1950." He often gave his
pictures numbers rather than names, because they weren't meant to be pictures
of things. Later a friend suggested "Lavender Mist" and the title stuck.

This painting was created by New York artist Jackson Pollock. It is made up of touches of blue, pink and gray, overlaid with a tangle of black and white streaks. The dense pattern creates a feeling of restless energy and movement.

Deliberate mess

Pollock made the picture by splattering and splashing paint onto a huge canvas laid flat on the floor. He dipped brushes in paint and flicked them at the canvas. Then he swung dribbling paint cans over it. The results might look messy, but Pollock insisted every spot and streak was deliberate. In his pictures, he claimed, "there is no accident."

About Pollock

Jackson Pollock was born in the United States in 1912. He went to New York to study art and soon became one of the city's leading artists. He was so famous for his messy, energetic way of painting that art critics gave him the nickname Jack the Dripper. He was killed in a car crash at the age of 44.

This photograph shows Pollock at work in his studio.

Splatter painting

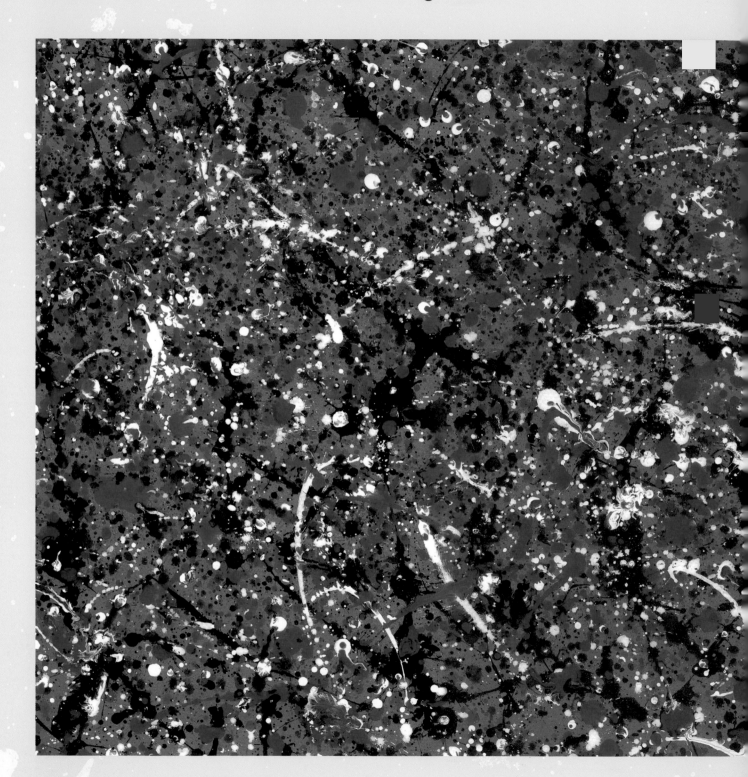

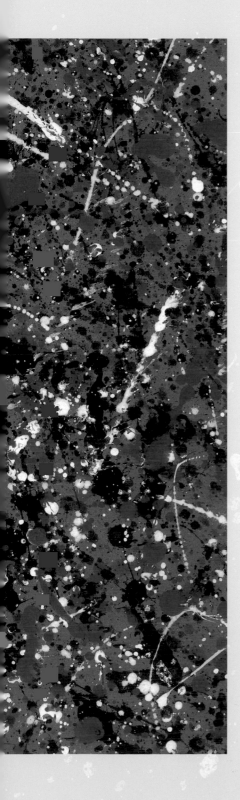

Jackson Pollock was famous for creating pictures out of splatters and splashes of paint – a method that's messy but fun to try yourself.

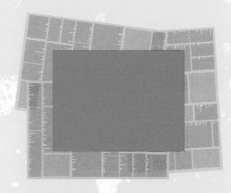

1. Spread out lots of old newspaper. Lay a piece of thick, colored paper on top of it.

2. Dilute some poster paint to make it runny. Dip in a brush, then shake it down sharply over the paper.

3. For fine spatters, dip a smaller brush in the paint. Holding it over the paper, flick the bristles, like this.

4. Do lots of shaking and flicking in different colors of paint, until the paper is full of spatters.

Glittering tiles

made by unknown artists in Iran between 1250 and 1300

These tiles are more than 700 years old, but the pictures are as sharp as if they were made yesterday.

These finely painted tiles form a pattern of stars and crosses, which fit together without any gaps. This is called tessellating. Although the shapes of the tiles repeat, the pictures on them don't. Each tile has a different arrangement of birds, animals and flowers.

Making tiles

Making tiles was a very skilled job. First, the artists shaped the tiles out of clay and baked them so the clay hardened. Then, they painted the tiles with special glazes (paints for clay) and baked them again, to make the glazes turn shiny. They used several kinds of glazes, including one mixed with tiny specks of metal. It's hard to see in a photograph, but the specks glitter in the light, creating a magical shimmering effect.

Tile style

In Iran and other countries in the Middle East, richly painted tiles cover many important buildings, both inside and out. The decoration is meant as a kind of celebration of everyday life.

The tiles on the left were made for a room in a palace. Palace tiles often include intricate pictures of animals, birds and people. Different styles of decoration, based on writing and geometric patterns, are used for tiles on religious buildings.

Specially made, elaborately decorated tiles cover entire buildings.

85

Sparkly tiles

The glittering Iranian tiles were decorated with specialized, glass-based glazes. But you can also get a sparkly "glazed" effect by using craft glue and glitter.

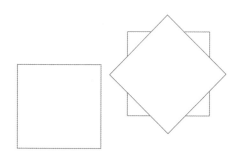

1. Cut three identical squares of cardboard. Overlap two of them to make a star shape.

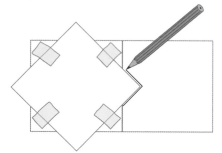

2. Tape the star together. Place the star along one edge of the third square and draw around the point.

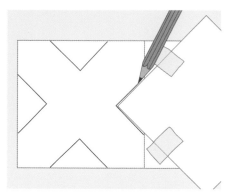

3. Do the same along each edge of the square, so you have the outline of a cross. Cut it out.

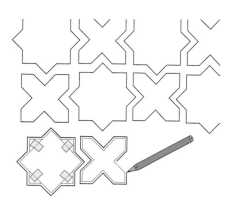

4. Place the cross and star onto a sheet of paper and draw around them. Do this until the paper is covered.

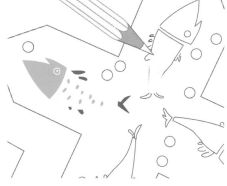

5. Draw animals and plants inside the paper shapes. Color them in with pencils or crayons.

6. Mix some craft glue with water and stir in a spoonful of glitter. Brush the glue all over the tiles.

When the glue is dry, cut out your tiles
and arrange them so that they tessellate.

the "Fighting Temeraire"

painted by Joseph Mallord William Turner in 1839

This painting shows a tug boat towing an old warship away for scrap. This was a real ship and a real event, as the picture's full title records – *The "Fighting Temeraire" Tugged to her Last Berth to be Broken Up, 1838.* The artist, Joseph Turner, had been among the crowds watching on the day.

Turner loved this picture. He called it his "darling" and refused to sell it.

Changing skies

Although Turner watched the *Temeraire* being towed away, he didn't paint exactly what he saw. He changed parts to make it look more dramatic. The old ship had lost its masts but he drew them in, exaggerating the contrast between the tall sailing ship and the squat, smoking tug. And, although it all happened in the morning, he set it against a glowing sunset, to create a feeling of something coming to an end.

About Turner

Joseph Mallord William Turner was born in England in 1775. A barber's son, he exhibited his first works in his father's shop. He hated publicity. As he became more famous, he hid behind a false name: Admiral Booth.

Stormy seas

Turner painted many atmospheric views of skies and seas. This project shows you how to paint your own stormy sea picture using watercolors – which Turner often used himself.

Use very watery paint and a wet brush.

1. Lightly sketch a ship in a storm on thick white paper. Fill in the ship, using a dark wax crayon.

2. Wipe a wet sponge over your paper. Then, mix some watercolor paint in pale blues and greens.

3. Brush streaks of blue and green diagonally all over the sea and sky. Let the streaks run together.

The salt makes watery marks.

4. Mix some watercolor paint in darker blues and greens. Streak it under the ship and across the sky.

5. Sprinkle patches of salt on top of the wet paint. Leave the picture to dry, then shake off the salt.

6. Use a white chalk pastel or chalk to add flecks of foam on the waves and lines of rain in the sky.

Mud Hand Circles

created by Richard Long in 1989

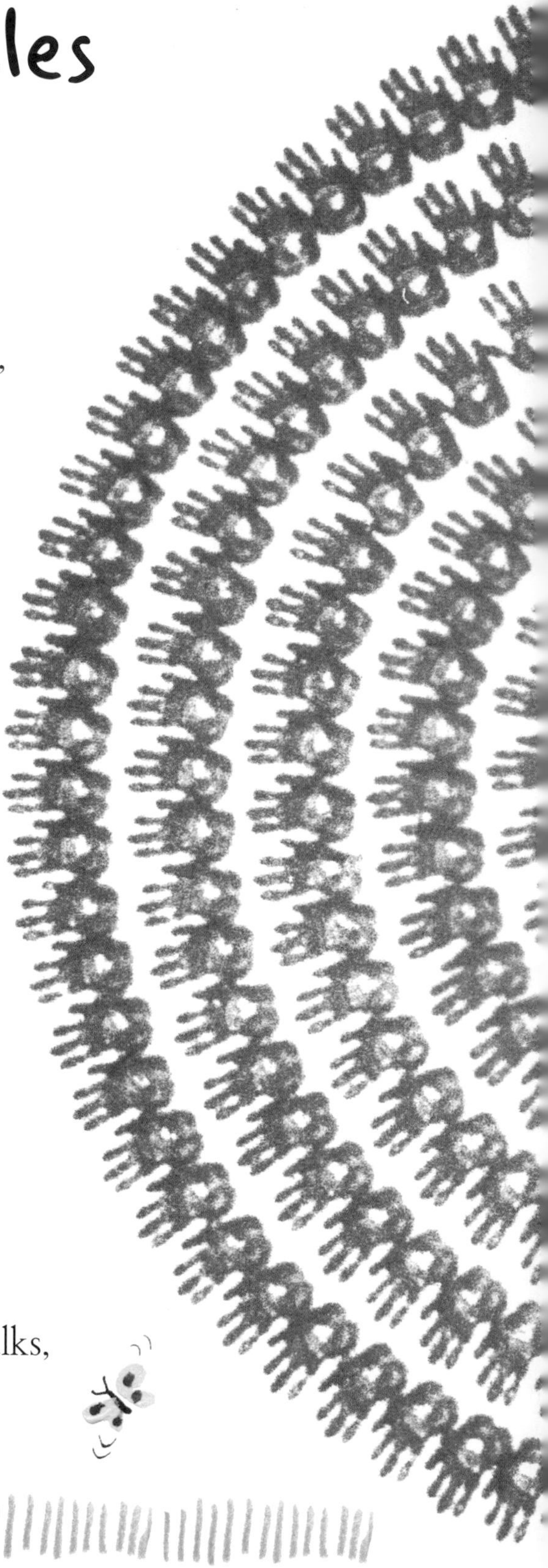

Handprints are one of the simplest, oldest ways for an artist to make a mark – in fact, the method dates back to prehistoric times. This huge modern picture shows hundreds of handprints, arranged in neat circles.

Mud pies

The artist, Richard Long, made this picture after going for a walk by the River Avon. Along the way, he gathered buckets of mud which he used to make these handprints on a whitewashed wall. The circles are so big, he had to stand on a ladder to finish them.

About Long

Richard Long was born in England in 1945. He is known for making art based on long country walks, and has even walked through the Arctic and the Himalayan Mountains. Sometimes, the walk is meant to be a work of art all by itself; sometimes, it is a hunt for materials to use.

This picture was created on the wall of a medieval hall in Jesus College, Cambridge, England.

One of Long's early works involved walking up and down a line of grass, and photographing the crushed stems.

93

Handprint circles

Richard Long made his handprint circles straight onto a wall. You probably won't be allowed to paint on a wall, so this project explains how to create handprint circles on paper.

Use a pencil.

1. Draw around a big plate on a big piece of paper. Squeeze some poster paint onto an old plate.

2. Press your hand flat into the paint. Then, press your hand onto the paper at the edge of the circle.

Wash your hand before each new color.

3. Squeeze different colors of paint onto more plates. Make more hand prints all around the circle.

4. Now, make another ring of hand prints inside the first. Leave a slight gap between the rings.

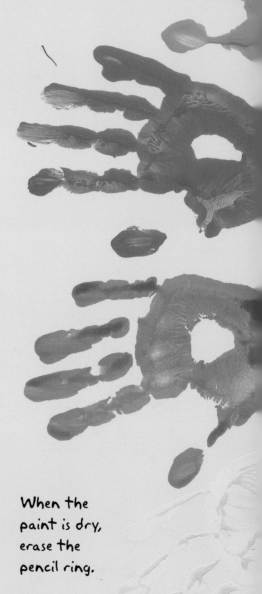

When the paint is dry, erase the pencil ring.

94

Every effort has been made to trace the copyright holders of the material in this book. If any rights have been omitted, the publishers offer their sincere apologies and will rectify this in any subsequent editions following notification. The publishers are grateful to the following organisations and individuals for their contributions and permission to reproduce material:

Cover: *The Starry Night* by van Gogh, see credit for pages 8-9. **Pages 6-7:** *Waterlilies – Morning* by Monet, see credit for pages 48-49. **Pages 8-9:** *The Starry Night* (1889) by van Gogh, oil on canvas, 74 x 92cm © (2006) The Museum of Modern Art (MoMA), New York/ Lillie P. Bliss Bequest/ Scala, Florence. **Pages 12-13:** *The Great Wave off Kanagawa* by Hokusai, color woodcut, 25 x 38cm © Historical Picture Archive/ CORBIS. **Pages 16-17:** *A Winter Scene with Skaters near a Castle* (c.1608-09) by Avercamp, oil on wood, 41 x 41cm © The National Gallery, London. **Pages 20-21:** *Punchinello with a Guitar* (1920) by Picasso, oil on canvas © Private Collection/ The Bridgeman Art Library/ Succession Picasso/ DACS 2006. Photograph of Picasso and his son Claude in 1955 © Bettmann/ CORBIS. **Pages 24-25:** *Songye Mask* (19th century) by an unknown artist, painted wood © The Art Archive/ Private Collection/ Dagli Orti (A). *Kuba Mask* (19th century) by an unknown artist, painted wood and straw © The Art Archive/ Private Collection/ Dagli Orti (A). **Pages 28-29:** *The Golden Fish* (1925) by Klee, oil and watercolor on paper and board, 50 x 69cm © Hamburger Kunsthalle, Hamburg, Germany/ The Bridgeman Art Library/ DACS 2006. **Pages 32-33:** *Monkeys in an Orange Grove* (1910) by Rousseau, oil on canvas, 111 x 163cm © Private Collection/ The Bridgeman Art Library. Photograph of Rousseau in his studio © Edimédia/ CORBIS. **Pages 36-37:** *Eleven Polychrome* (1956) by Calder, sheet metal, wire and paint © Christie's Images/ CORBIS/ Estate of Alexander Calder/ ARS, NY and DACS, London 2006. **Pages 40-41:** *The Sorrows of the King* (1952) by Matisse, gouache on canvas, 292 x 386cm © Museé National d'Art Moderne, Centre Pompidou, Paris, France/ The Bridgeman Art Library/ Succession H. Matisse/ DACS 2006. Photograph of Matisse © akg-images/ Bianconero. **Pages 44-45:** *Nocturne in Black and Gold, the Falling Rocket* (c.1875) by Whistler, oil on wood, 60 x 47cm © The Detroit Institute of Arts, USA/ Gift of Dexter M. Ferry Jr./ The Bridgeman Art Library. **Pages 48-49:** *Waterlilies – Morning* centre right section (1914-18) by Monet, oil on canvas, 200 x 425cm © Museé de l'Orangerie, Paris, France/ Lauros/ Giraudon/ The Bridgeman Art Library. **Pages 52-53:** *Squares with Concentric Circles* (1913) by Kandinsky, watercolor, gouache and black chalk, 24 x 32cm © ARTOTHEK/ ADAGP, Paris and DACS, London 2006. **Pages 56-57:** *Cat* (1747) by Shen Quan, ink on paper © Christie's Images/ CORBIS. Brush strokes by Evelyn Ong. **Pages 60-61:** *Dancers in Blue* (c.1897) by Degas, pastel on paper © Archivo Iconografico, S.A./ CORBIS. **Pages 64-65:** *The Square* (1948-49) by Giacometti, bronze, 59 x 45 x 25cm © Private Collection/ Lefevre Fine Art Ltd., London/ The Bridgeman Art Library/ ADAGP, Paris and DACS, London 2006. **Pages 68-69:** *beautiful, sharp, screaming, subtle, ice-cream-ish, yikes, gosh with pinks painting (with rosy orange center)* (1995) by Hirst, gloss household paint on canvas, 214cm diameter © Damien Hirst, courtesy Jay Jopling/ White Cube (London). **Pages 72-73:** *Bark painting* by Bulunbulun © Penny Tweedie/ CORBIS/ VISCOPY, Australia/ DACS 2006. **Pages 76-77:** *Jimson Weed* (1932) by O'Keeffe, oil on canvas, 122 x 102cm © (2006) The Georgia O'Keefe Museum, Santa Fe/ Dono della Fondazione Burnett/ Fondazione Georgia O'Keefe/ Art Resource/ Scala, Florence/ ARS, NY and DACS, London 2006. **Pages 80-81:** *Lavender Mist* (1950) by Pollock, oil, enamel and aluminium paint on canvas, 221 x 300cm © National Gallery of Art, Washington DC, USA/ The Bridgeman Art Library/ ARS, NY and DACS, London 2006. Photograph of Pollock © Time & Life Pictures/ Getty Images. **Pages 84-85:** *Wall panel of star- and cross-shaped tiles depicting birds, animals and figures, Islamic, from Kashan in Central Iran* (c.1250-1300) by unknown artists, 79 x 50cm © Louvre, Paris, France/ Peter Willi/ The Bridgeman Art Library. **Pages 88-89:** *The Fighting Temeraire* (1839) by Turner, oil on canvas, 91 x 122cm © The National Gallery, London. **Pages 92-93:** *Mud Hand Circles* (1989) by Long, 320cm diameter, courtesy of the artist and Haunch of Venison, photograph by kind permission of the Master and Fellows, Jesus College, Cambridge.